The Little Gift Book of

OREGON

Whitecap Books
Vancouver/Toronto

Second Printing 1998

Text by Elaine Jones
Edited by Linda Ostrowalker
Cover and interior design by Carolyn Deby
Cover photograph by Steve Short
Typography by CompuType, Vancouver, B.C., Canada

Printed and bound in Canada by Friesens Corporation
Altona, Manitoba

Canadian Cataloguing in Publication Data
Jones, Elaine.
  Little gift book of Oregon

  ISBN 1-55110-056-8

  1. Oregon—Pictorial works. I. Title.
F877.J65 1993   979.5′043′0222 C93-091147-4

Contents

*Oregon's fresh produce is celebrated in
annual festivals throughout the state.*

Oregon

Like residents of most states, Oregonians are filled with pride about the beauties of their corner of the universe. Visitors to Oregon readily agree that here nature has been particularly abundant in natural gifts, giving freely of a ruggedly beautiful coastline, several distinctive mountain ranges, spectacular rivers, and even seaside sand dunes and a high desert.

Oregon's northern boundary with Washington is defined by the powerful Columbia River, one of the continent's major arteries. The magnificent Snake River and its canyon mark most of Oregon's eastern border with Idaho. To the south are Nevada and California, and to the west the open Pacific.

Running roughly north-south and defining much of Oregon's character is the Cascade Range, part of a continuous mountain chain that spans the continent from Mexico to Alaska. The Cascades include a string of volcanic peaks, including Mount Jefferson, the Three Sisters, and the state's highest, Mount Hood. At 11,235 feet, it dominates the surrounding area and can be seen from the hills of Portland. Between the Cascades and the sea is the Coast Range—low-lying mountains with a maximum elevation of about 4,000 feet. West of the Cascades, the warm, moisture-laden air of the Pacific

Left: *Smith Rock State Park, on the Crooked River.*

3

and a temperate climate foster exuberant growth; the tall timbers that grow thickly on the slopes are the basis of Oregon's timber industry. The fertile valleys of the Willamette, Rogue, and Umpqua rivers form the major population base for Oregon and are prime fruit, vegetable, wine-producing, and dairy regions.

East of the Cascades, the climate and topography change dramatically. On the leeward side of the mountains, drier pine forests give way to the high, arid country of the interior plateau. In northeastern Oregon, the Blue and Wallowa mountains rise from the plateau, a wilderness of jagged snow-covered peaks interspersed with clear alpine lakes. To the southeast is the high desert, characterized by rolling sagebrush hills, ephemeral alkaline lakes, deeply incised canyons, and isolated mountain ranges. Eastern Oregon is "big country," with plenty of room for ranching and wheat farming.

Oregon's diversity is its greatest strength, and that extends to its communities, which range from its largest city, Portland, with a metropolitan population of 1.5 million, to its mid-sized cities and the many small centers in rural areas. Even the largest cities are known for their sense of "neighborliness," and local festivities range from Ashland's famous Shakespeare Festival to rodeos, such as the week-long extravaganza at Pendleton, and countless agricultural and musical events.

Oregonians are also proud of their history. It was the Oregon Trail, a tortuous two-thousand-mile route from Missouri that brought the first intrepid pioneers to the West. A variety of sites, such as historic gold-mining towns and the campsites of Lewis and Clark on their epic voyage of discovery down the Columbia River are designated national historic sites. But it is the land—formed by ancient seas, fiery volcanic eruptions, and erosion—that is Oregon's most compelling feature. Museums, national monuments, parks, and wildlife refuges protect ecologically important areas and explain the geological forces that created this unique state.

Rocky shoreline near Depoe Bay.

The Coast

One of the world's most scenic and unspoiled routes winds for some four hundred miles along the Oregon coast. For lovers of wild seascapes, there is nothing quite so spectacular as this highway, which hugs the shore for most of its length. Here, the power of the Pacific has gnawed away at the land, creating a world of craggy headlands, sandy beaches, and the distinctive sea-carved pinnacles known as seastacks. Wherever there is a protected cove (and there are relatively few on this open coastline), fishing fleets are tucked away, ready to harvest the great riches of the Pacific: chinook, perch, flounder, and steelhead.

Many tours of the Oregon coast start at the historic city of Astoria, named for its founder, John Jacob Astor, and the site of the first European settlement in Oregon. Usually regarded as a coastal city even though it is actually several miles up the wide mouth of the Columbia River, Astoria is linked by a four-mile-long bridge to Washington State.

South of Astoria, there is a string of charming oceanside settlements, but Cannon Beach stands out because of its strong artistic component, a beach that stretches for seven miles, and the picturesque rock formations

Left: *Lighthouse at Hecata Head.*

offshore. Imposing, 235-foot-tall Haystack Rock, surrounded by smaller stacks called the Needles, is a wildfowl refuge and a favorite subject for photographers.

Protected places on this open coastline are well utilized, no matter how tiny they are, and Depoe Bay claims the title of the world's smallest navigable harbor. Just six acres in size, the harbor is separated from the open Pacific by a narrow, rocky channel that must be carefully navigated. Perched at the edge of the Pacific—its main street is the bridge that crosses the access channel—the town is imbued with a strong maritime flavor.

With every turn of the road revealing another beautiful viewpoint, it is impossible to pick one site that surpasses the rest. But from the 800-foot-high cliffs of Cape Perpetua, the highest vantage point on the coast, the view is heartstopping. A visitor center, nature trails, and a twenty-two-mile loop drive introduce visitors to the natural forces at work, from tide pools to cliff erosion. Just a few miles south of here, nature's astounding variety is demonstrated when the landscape changes from the solidity of towering cliffs to shifting, malleable dunes. The Oregon Dunes National Recreation Area stretches for forty-seven miles, from just south of Florence to Coos Bay. Covering an area of fourteen thousand acres, some of the dunes reach heights of five hundred feet. According to geologists, the dunes were created when a volcanic shelf of pumice and ash escaped the lava flow. Washed into the sea, the sand was brought back by the tides and blown ashore by westerly winds, a constant process that saw the dunes gradually increase in size. When they encroach upon highways and rivers, forest vegetation is planted to stop their progress. Sculpted by the wind into wave-shapes, the dunes are a magical world of sea, sky, and sand.

South of the dunes, the landscape becomes more rugged and the beaches less explored. This southern portion of the coast boasts mild temperatures year-round, and near Brookings, just a few miles from the California border, a short hike leads to a stand of redwoods.

The Oregon Dunes National Recreation Area.

Old homes in Astoria, the first European settlement in Oregon.

The surf rolls in at Cannon Beach.

Sea Lion Caves, a unique mainland refuge for Steller's sea lions.

Pebble beach at Yaquina Head, near Newport.

Tidal rocks, Bandon Beach.

Surf pounds the rugged shoreline at Cape Kiwanda.

Looking north from Seal Rock to Ona Beach.

A mild climate and heavy rainfall promote lush growth on the Oregon coast.

The main street of Cannon Beach.

Colorful rocks at Beverly Beach near Newport.

Harbor seals bask on the rocks near Bandon.

A Pacific sunset near Lincoln City.

The South

Oregon's southern region encompasses a wide variety of terrain—forested hills, lush valleys, the state's largest lake, mountain ranges with elevations from one thousand to ten thousand feet, wetlands, and the dry tablelands that mark the beginning of the Great Basin area of southern Oregon.

Interstate Highway 5 links the major population centers of the Umpqua and Rogue river valleys. Rising in the Cascades and flowing to the Pacific, the valleys enjoy the sunny, drier climate of the leeward side of the Coast and Siskiyou mountains. Wine-tasting tours, roadside fruit and vegetable stands, and produce festivals attest to the productivity of the valleys, while the wild and scenic Rogue River is also famed for its whitewater rafting and its legendary runs of steelhead.

One of Oregon's most fascinating geographic features is located in this region at the crest of the Cascade Range. Crater Lake had its beginnings about 6800 years ago when 12,000-foot Mount Mazama exploded in an eruption a hundred times more powerful than that of Mount St. Helens. Virtually all life in the area was extinguished and volcanic ash fell half an inch deep as far away as Saskatchewan, Canada. The caldera, five miles wide, gradu-

Left: *Ponderosa pines at Klamath Falls.*

23

ally filled with meltwater, creating the deepest lake in the United States, at 1,932 feet. In places its walls rise another two thousand feet from the lake level. The purity and great depth of the lake accounts for its intense blue color. Oregon's only national park, Crater Lake is a favorite with hikers and skiers, and a well-used trail system leads to stunning views of the lake rim and surrounding peaks. The indigenous plant life of the Cascades has repopulated almost everywhere but the Pumice Desert, where volcanic debris fell to a depth of two hundred feet and cannot hold enough moisture to support life.

The Oregon Caves National Monument reveals more of the earth's mysterious workings. Located in the Siskiyou Mountains, the lava and limestone formations form a complex network of caverns and passageways that have been molded over eons into fantastic shapes. The caves were declared a national monument by President Taft in 1909 and they continue to attract many visitors each year with guided tours of the underground chambers.

Upper Klamath Lake is Oregon's largest natural lake. This shallow lake is part of a string of lakes and marshes that collectively form the Klamath Basin. These wetlands are protected nesting grounds and the area is an important stop for wildfowl on the Pacific Flyway. Six wildlife refuges have been established here, each with its own distinctive habitat. More than two hundred bird species have been identified in the area, including white pelicans with their nine-foot wingspans.

Klamath Falls, at the south end of Upper Klamath Lake, is the jumping-off point for hikers, anglers, and cross-country skiers exploring the fabulous alpine recreational wilderness west and north of here. Hundreds of pristine alpine lakes are hidden among the hemlock-covered slopes of the Mountain Lakes Wilderness Area west of Upper Klamath and the Sky Lakes Wilderness south of Crater Lake.

*Pelican Lake, Pelican Butte and
Klamath Lake viewed from 9,495-foot
Mount McLoughlin.*

*Japanese maple at the entrance to Lithia
Park, Ashland.*

Wizard Island on Crater Lake, formed
by the ancient eruption of Mount
Mazama.

Shakespeare Festival, Ashland.

Rogue Gorge, Rogue River, near Union Creek.

Historic building, Jacksonville.

*Several wineries near Roseburg
participate in wine-tasting tours.*

The Southeast

The high desert area of southeastern Oregon is the least-populated and least-known part of the state. To some, the highway runs through mile after mile of what seems to be tediously similar terrain: dusty sagebrush plains broken by brown hills in the distance. To others, this is treasured "big country," where settlements are few and far between and nature has been little disturbed. Off the beaten track, there are dramatic escarpments and deep canyons, and to the discerning eye, the subtle beauty of the desert is to be found everywhere.

The major center in the southeast is Burns, at the intersection of the three main highways. Near Burns is the Malheur National Wildlife Refuge on Malheur Lake, which, during wet seasons, is one of the largest lakes in the Pacific Northwest. The refuge covers 153,000 acres and is best seen by vehicle; a stopover for birds on the Pacific Flyway, spring and fall bring a wide variety of migrating birds, including snow geese and sandhill cranes, which add to the resident bird population. Malheur and the Hart Mountain National Antelope Refuge to the west, which is unique in the United States, are essential oases for wildlife. However, during periods of drought the lakes

Left: *Steens Mountain.*

and marshes can dry up completely, driving away the abundant wildlife that usually frequent these high desert oases.

One of the dramatic formations in this region is Steens Mountain, a monolithic block created along a fault line in the earth's crust. From the west, the 9700-foot Steens presents a more or less gradual slope, but the eastern face falls almost vertically to the Alvord Desert a mile below. A circular road leads from the 4000-foot level to the ridge, a trip that is well worthwhile, particularly in spring, when wildflowers and alpine grasses carpet the slopes. Those who are fortunate may see wild horses, bighorn sheep, and antelope.

The canyons and rock formations of the high desert draw a particular kind of outdoors enthusiast: those who seek challenge and adventure far from civilization. Formed by erosion over millennia, these starkly beautiful waterways are navigable only for a short season and are subject to extremes of temperature. The Owyhee River, at the eastern edge of the state, is considered Oregon's wildest whitewater river: its exciting rapids and steep gorges are restricted to those in the expert category. The passage carved by the river cuts through layers of compacted volcanic ash, and at the Honeycombs, east of the Owyhee reservoir, weak spots in the rock have been eroded into caves, ledges, and round indentations.

This area is also the haunt of rockhounds. Rich in agates, jasper, and petrified wood, Nyssa is known as the "Thunderegg Capital of Oregon" and hosts an annual five-day rockhound festival.

In a state that abounds in spectacular geological features, Fort Rock, in the northwestern corner of this region, is considered one of the most unusual. Here the circular crater of an ancient volcano rises out of the surrounding dry sagebrush hills. Almost half a mile in diameter, it is a ghostly reminder of ages past. A few miles away, Hole in Ground, a circular crater about five hundred feet deep, is the result of the massive explosion near Fort Rock.

Downhill skiing at Warner Canyon Ski Area.

Cyclists on Steens Mountain.

*The high desert region, with Steens
Mountain in the background.*

*A nighthawk perches on a fencepost
near Malheur National Wildlife Refuge.*

Malheur Lake at dawn, near Burns.

The Northeast

Here, in Oregon's northeast corner, can be found the most pristine and diverse areas of the state. Marking its eastern border is North America's deepest gorge, 6,600-foot-deep Hells Canyon on the Snake River. To the south and west is the John Day River, which drains the dry canyonlands of eastern Oregon; fossil beds along the river record a fascinating history of life over many millennia. Between lie the Blue and Wallowa mountains, the Wallowas, high jagged peaks soaring above the timberline, the larger Blue Mountain range less rugged, with gentler forested slopes. Lightly populated and hard to reach, these areas afford a paradise for anglers, backpackers, and other wilderness buffs. In the Columbia plateau, centering on Pendleton, the rugged mountains give way to farm- and ranchlands rich in history.

Oregon's vast northeastern region is bisected by Interstate Highway 84, which parallels the famous Oregon Trail, the overland route that led the first settlers to the coast. In some places along the historic route, ruts worn by the wagon trains can still be seen. Farewell Bend State Park, on the Snake River, marks the spot where the wagon trains turned west toward the Columbia, to head northwest over the Blue Mountains, the most difficult terrain

Left: *A rainbow graces rolling pastureland in Grant County.*

of the trip. Monuments and roadside markers tell about the trail, and just outside the city of Baker, an interpretive center explains the rigors of yesterday's travelers to today's visitors.

Baker is also the gateway to the Hells Canyon National Recreation Area. Covering 652,000 acres in Oregon and Idaho, it has long been known to backpackers, hunters, anglers, and skiers, but its distance from major population centers ensures that those who seek solitude can always find it. The heart of the recreation area, Hells Canyon on the Snake River, is a thousand feet deeper than Colorado's Grand Canyon. From the rim, the vastness of the view overwhelms the sense of the river, a white ribbon far below. But at river level, its immense power and the multitude of rapids are a challenge for the most expert rafters.

After the 3,615-foot elevation of Deadman's Pass, there is a descent to the rolling wheatfields of the Columbia plateau. Irrigated with deep wells and river water, this has become Oregon's most productive ranching and wheat farming country. As well as the working ranches, recreational dude ranches capitalize on the ambience of the region, offering city slickers a chance to go fishing, hunting, and riding. The world-famous Pendleton Round-Up, held in September, is a week-long rodeo extravaganza celebrating the ranching heritage of the area.

The John Day River meanders through the arid tablelands of eastern Oregon before turning north on its journey to the Columbia. Three separate units form the John Day Fossil Beds National Monuments—the Sheep Rock Unit near Dayville, the Painted Hills Unit near Mitchell, and the Clarno Unit near Fossil. Colorful rock formations, fossilized bones, and imprints tell the story of how these dry, sagebrush-covered hills evolved over several million years from huge inland seas with a subtropical climate, each unit highlighting a different aspect of this evolution.

Flowering grass near Baker.

Pete's Point in the Wallowa Mountains.

*Abandoned farm in the Wallowa
Mountains.*

Fields near Pendleton.

Mount Emily, north of La Grande.

*Fertile valleys nestle between the snow-
capped peaks of the Wallowa Mountains.*

Hurricane Creek, Wallowa Mountains.

The Matterhorn, 9,845 feet, seen from Mount Sacajawea.

*Joseph Canyon, in the Wallowa
Mountains.*

Central Oregon

Central Oregon is ski country—amongst the best in the Northwest. On the lee side of the Cascades, the weather is clear and sunny, with relatively little precipitation at lower levels and abundant snowfall in the mountains. But, typical of the diversity found throughout the entire state, there are also productive forests, cattle ranches, and wheatfields. High desert country can also be found here.

Nestled on the eastern slopes of the Cascades, Bend is the largest city in central Oregon and the hub of a wide variety of recreational pursuits in the mountains. Mount Bachelor, twenty-two miles west, is a mecca for skiers. One of the most popular ski areas in the Northwest and ranked among the top nationally, it has outstanding views of the surrounding peaks, a 3,100-foot vertical drop from its 9,065-foot summit, and extensive cross-country trails. But skiing isn't the only attraction around Bend: to its east and south are the equally fascinating sights of the high desert.

Just east of Bend, a whole different world opens up. Ancient lava flows, stunted junipers, and sand dunes formed by ash from the ancient eruptions of Mount Mazama and Mount Newberry create a desert wilderness of unusual

Left: *Rock climbing at Smith Rock State Park.*

beauty. South of here, 56,000-acre Newberry National Volcanic Monument encompasses lava flows, lakes, and pine forests. The five-mile-wide caldera of the ancient Newberry volcano holds two lakes—known for their excellent fishing—and features several obsidian flows. Trails take in the geological sights, such as the Lava Cast Forest, formed some six thousand years ago when the eruption of Mount Newberry poured molten lava over a ponderosa pine forest. The trees burned or rotted away, but their forms were preserved by the hardened lava "casts." A road leads to the 7,985-foot crest of Paulina Peak, which allows far-reaching views of the caldera, with the snow-capped Cascades and Fort Rock in the distance.

Smith Rocks State Park attracts many outdoor enthusiasts, but it has also developed an international reputation with climbers. The vertical, 300-foot walls of the sandstone canyon glow with warm yellows and oranges, contrasting beautifully with the green banks of the Crooked River below. Climbers practice their skills on more than two hundred marked routes.

To the west, towering over the eastern plateau, is the high lakes region of the Cascades. Three wilderness areas—Mount Jefferson, Mount Washington, and Three Sisters—preserve a huge wilderness playground of imposing peaks, rivers, forests, canyons, and evidence of volcanic activity, such as smaller cinder cones and pumice fields.

Three Sisters has been described as Oregon's most-visited wilderness area. It boasts many superlatives: the three volcanic peaks, all over 10,000 feet high, the state's largest glaciers, and Oregon's highest lake, Teardrop Pool. While some of the lakes and outlooks are well used, it is easy to get off the beaten path and find true solitude in this immense wilderness, where drifting ice can be seen in glacier-surrounded lakes such as Chambers Lake, which is located at an altitude of seven thousand feet. For those seeking a challenge, the Pacific Crest Trail traverses the Three Sisters wilderness for fifty-two miles.

Several communities host rodeos through the summer months.

*South Sister, in the Three Sisters
wilderness area.*

The Crooked River.

Majestic Mount Jefferson, 10,499 feet.

The Warm Springs Indian Reservation.

Downhill skiing at Mount Bachelor.

White River Falls.

Mount Hood and the Columbia River Gorge

The Columbia River, which forms most of Oregon's northern boundary with Washington, is one of the most powerful and scenic waterways on the continent. Acknowledging the beauty of the Columbia Gorge, where the river cuts its swath through the Cascades, the area between Troutdale and the Deschutes River was accorded National Scenic Waterway status in 1986, a move that will protect the remaining natural areas of the river from further development. In a state that boasts many extraordinarily beautiful areas, the Columbia Gorge is without peer.

The river is also of great historic significance. Used for centuries by native Americans, it provided early overland explorers Lewis and Clark with a route to the coast. The Lewis and Clark State Park near Troutdale commemorates their historic 1805 expedition. During this century, the power of the river has been harnessed by six major dams providing hydroelectric power for two states. Today highways parallel the river on both sides, and development has changed the river significantly, yet the Columbia and its gorge remain one of Oregon's most beautiful areas.

Interstate Highway 84 is a rapid and efficient roadway at river level, but

Left: *Wahkeenah Falls.*

the old Columbia River Highway allows a leisurely look at the sights of the river from the rim of the gorge. Built in 1915, it was considered a miracle of modern engineering at the time and is still a fabulous drive. One of the most notable features of the Columbia Gorge is the profusion of waterfalls formed by tributary streams that cascade over the cliffs. The double cascades of Multnomah Falls make it the highest in the state, at 620 feet, but there are more than twenty other major falls, most accessible by short trails.

At Bonneville, visitors can see the first dam constructed on the Columbia. From the riverside park, it's possible to watch watercraft pass through the navigation lock and see how fish ladders allow salmon to pass the dam on their annual migrations.

Dominating the entire region is Mount Hood, Oregon's tallest mountain at 11,235 feet. Its distinctive volcanic cone is snowcapped year-round, and avid skiers can continue their sport even in the summer at the Palmer Snowfield's 8,500-foot elevation. Probably the most accessible mountain in the Cascades, it attracts huge numbers of skiers, hikers, campers, and climbers, thousands of whom attempt the summit each year. The forty-mile Timberline Trail, a rugged five-day hike for backpackers, circles the mountain, passing through a series of stunning alpine meadows and permanent snowfields. The most recently active of Oregon's volcanic Cascade Mountains, Hood has experienced minor eruptions as recently as the 1800s, and south of the summit hikers might encounter steam vents and hot rocks.

Well used in winter and summer, Mount Hood is the center of the Mount Hood National Forest, over a million acres in area. Its northern face descends to the fertile Hood River valley. Oregon's largest apple-growing region, the valley also produces pears and cherries. A favorite drive is the circle route, which heads southeast from Portland to Mount Hood, then turns north through the Hood River valley, returning along the Columbia Gorge.

Windsurfing at Hood River.

At 11,245 feet, Mount Hood's distinctive peak dominates the surrounding area.

Crown Point on the Columbia Gorge.

*Ramona Falls, in the Mount Hood
National Forest.*

A full moon adds to the beauty of the Columbia Gorge.

*Climbers on Eliot Glacier, on the north
side of Mount Hood.*

*Mount Hood reflected in the tranquil
waters of Lost Lake.*

*A path through the forest near Portland
Trail, Columbia Gorge.*

Multnomah Falls, second-highest in the country, plummets 620 feet.

Portland and the Willamette Valley

Long, wide, and fertile, cradled between the Coast Mountains and the Cascades, Oregon's Willamette Valley is the most populous area of the state. Settled a century ago by westward-bound pioneers on the Oregon Trail, the valley today is a pastiche of farms, small rural communities, the state's largest and second largest cities, Portland and Eugene, and its capital, Salem.

Home to some 1.5 million people, Portland manages to retain a small-town charm that is at least in part due to its lovely setting. At the confluence of the Columbia and Willamette rivers, the city is blessed with a mild climate year-round, attested to by lush private gardens and numerous public parks—160 of them, including the largest urban park in an American city, Forest Park. To the west are the Coast Range mountains in the distance; to the east, Mount Scott and Mount Tabor rise out of the valley plain, with the Cascades beyond—Rainier, Adams, and St. Helens in Washington; Hood and Jefferson in Oregon.

Although far from the sea, Portland is one of the most active ports on the West Coast, its busy terminals handling shipments of grain, lumber, ore, and automobiles. The Willamette River divides the city roughly in half on

Left: *Forecourt fountain at night, Portland.*

75

an east-west basis. Since 1967, the river has been the focus of a far-sighted conservation and reclamation program. The fish have now returned to its once-polluted waters, and Portland residents can swim, boat, and fish right within the city limits. Portland is also noted for its architecture, a skillful blend of old and new, with two nationally designated historic areas containing sensitively restored buildings and award-winning modern-day architecture.

Within a few minutes of downtown Portland, along its western edge, is a feature unique among large cities: over 5,300 acres in parks. Forest Park, almost 5,000 acres of tall timber left largely in its natural condition, has miles of hiking trails. Other parks include Hoyt Arboretum, with public lectures and tours; Japanese Garden, a serene haven in the bustle of the city; Washington Park International Rose Test Garden, with over four hundred varieties of rose in bloom from May to September; and Washington Park Zoo, which highlights wildlife from around the world.

Situated in the heart of the valley, Salem is one of the state's oldest cities. The white marble capitol building, the old Reed Opera House, and Willamette University are evidence of the long tradition of this gracious city, first settled in 1834. Throughout the valley, covered bridges, venerable farms, and historic buildings date back to the days of the Oregon Trail, when the Willamette was the main north-south artery and small settlements sprang up along its length at mills and shipping points.

Its tall timbers have given the lower Willamette Valley claim to the "Timber Capital of the World" title. Eugene, which grew up around the lumber industry, is today the center of a rapidly expanding wine-producing region. Like other communities along the Willamette, Eugene has taken advantage of its setting and established many parks along the banks of the river, where cyclists and joggers can enjoy miles of traffic-free trails.

Portland's beautiful gardens thrive in the mild climate.

State Capitol Building, Salem.

Pioneer Square in Portland.

Visitors can tour the twenty-two rooms of Portland's Pittock Mansion.

Portlandia, *one of the many works of art to be seen throughout Portland.*

Campus of Portland State University.

Gates of Portland's Chinatown.

Tea house at the Japanese Gardens, Portland.

Aerial view of downtown Portland.

Falls in the Willamette River watershed.

The International Rose Test Gardens,
Portland.

The peaceful Willamette Valley.

Portland at night with Mount Hood in the background.

Salmon Fountain, Portland.

A country road near Hillsboro.

Photo Credits